JIMMY VEE & TRAVIS MILLER

"Jim and Travis have a very unique way of expressing themselves. They have a sincerity that's honest and they have a method that's proven."

—*Greg McCoy, Roper Kia*

"Jimmy and Travis are inspirational and brilliant. Hold on and get ready for the ride."

—*Mike Guizar, Michaels Car Center*

"Eccentric, quirky and outside of the box. I think all those things describe Jimmy and Travis."

—*Tracy Myers, Frank Myers Auto Maxx*

"Being attractive is hard work unless you can ignore the bad advice given you every day. Marketers by nature don't want to learn anything new, so the few of us who anxiously grab at new thinkers make all the money. That's where Vee and Miller come in, with their Ineffective Ruts Be Damned philosophy. Whoever has the balls to put into practice what it takes to be "gravitational" will get his money's worth and more."

—*Richard Laermer, Author, Full Frontal PR*

"*Gravitational Marketing* takes lofty ideas to even greater heights."

—Jay Conrad Levinson, "The Father of Guerrilla Marketing" and the author of the *Guerrilla Marketing* series of books

Jimmy and Travis have done it again. This book is a challenge to the dealer community to wake up and rethink who is in control. Profit is not a 4-letter word, and your enemy is a wolf in sheep's clothing; this book strips away the cloak and exposes them. The rules of marketing have changed and you will find timely, concise and usable tips to bring fun and profitably back to the auto industry.

—Peter "Web Doc" Martin, Cactus Sky Communications

"*Gravitational Marketing* cuts through all the hype and misinformation often surrounding good marketing practices and gives you a roadmap to achieving measurable success. I strongly recommend it."

—Joseph Sugarman, BluBlocker Sunglass Corporation

"No entrepreneur can achieve massive success without a lot of marketing savvy. However, most of what is written about marketing is by academics. While it may sound good, it's of no help at all as the authors have never been in the trenches. *Gravitational Marketing* is completely different. You are offered lots of proven techniques to become more successful by 'street smart' authors who walk the talk—Jimmy Vee & Travis Miller. You can immediately put these to use."

—Ted Nicholas, Author of *Billion Dollar Marketing Secrets*

"Finally a book that gives the REAL secret. Attraction comes from working, not waiting. If you're looking to attract wealth, if you're looking to attract success, even if you're looking to attract more sales, this is a book that will give you a formula that will actually work. It's not a secret, it's an action."

—Jeffrey Gitomer, Author of *The New York Times* best sellers
The Sales Bible, The Little Red Book of Selling, The Little Black Book of Connections, and *The Little Gold Book of YES! Attitude*.

"*Gravitational Marketing* lays out a compelling case for a better approach and tells you everything you need to know about the science of attraction. But first you must dare yourself to be unconventional."

—David Meerman Scott, Bestselling Author of *The New Rules of Marketing & PR*

"*Gravitational Marketing* is about creating irresistible attraction, but in your marketing and not just your personal magnetism. You'll find out how to make you, your company and your products and services attractive to customers without pounding them over the head. *Gravitational Marketing* is a doorway to the next step in the evolution of marketing."

—Kevin Hogan, Psy.D., Author of *Irresistible Attraction: Secrets of Personal Magnetism* and *The Science of Influence*

For our new sons, Quinn Emerson and Vincent Chase—

an amazing adventure awaits you both.

"Do or do not. There is no try."

—Yoda, *Empire Strikes Back*

INVASION
OF THE PROFIT
SNATCHERS

A **Practical Guide** To **Increasing Sales Without Cutting Prices** & **Protecting Your Dealership** From Looters, Moochers & Vendors Gone Wild

Jimmy Vee & Travis Miller

ATLAS
PRESS

Published by Atlas Press, LLC, Orlando, Florida.

Invasion of the Profit Snatchers: A Practical Guide To Increasing Sales Without Cutting Prices & Protecting Your Dealership From Looters, Moochers & Vendors Gone Wild

FIRST EDITION

ISBN: 978-0-9854782-0-9
Library of Congress Control Number: 2012907237

Cover design by Plinio Tejeda
Illustrations by Daniel Burke

Gravitational Marketing® and Rich Dealers® are registered trademarks of Scend LLC.

Printed in the United States of America.

10 9 8 7 6 5 4 3 2

TABLE OF CONTENTS

ACKNOWLEDGMENTS

Our deepest gratitude goes to these fine people:

Rob Berkley, who opened our eyes.

Jamey Holder, who keeps us pointed forward.

The original RDs, who believed in us before others did.

All RDs, who trust us now and keep the revolution alive.

Our VIPs—Tom, Jill, Kevin, Marvin, who keep us sharp.

Donna Fuller, Plinio Tejeda and Faith Alexander, who helped turn our crazy idea into a book.

All our dedicated ESPers, who know the true value of worthwhile work.

Our "elite" network—Charlie, Rob, Chris, Adam, Brian, Michael, Bob, Bill, Mike, Darren, Robert, Chris, Andrew, Matt, John, Victor, Dave, who push us.

Our parents, who did it right.

Our wives, who love us anyway.

CHAPTER 1:

THE INVASION IS UNDERWAY

They're here to take your money. They're here to destroy your business. This is bad.

These days being a car dealer is *rough*. The government keeps piling on regulations and red tape. Customers want every car below invoice. The media has convinced the public you're ripping people off. The manufacturers believe it would be a better business if it weren't for all you *pesky dealers*. It seems impossible to find good help that you can trust. Rising fuel prices, dwindling used car supplies, technology-forced "transparency" and the endless maze of new high-tech tools that, for the most part, seem to slow things down rather than speed things up...it all makes this business less fun, less rewarding, less fulfilling, less lucrative and less interesting than ever before.

What's worse, even many vendors, who presumably should be on your side, to whom dealers pay small fortunes, are on a mission to eliminate dealers from the landscape (and why not...they figure they can hijack your profit as their own). Dealers are viewed as middlemen who extract profit without adding value. If they had their druthers, people would buy cars from a web site (maybe it would be called www.carmazon.com). There would be free two day shipping, financing arranged through Visa, virtual test drives. And then nine out of ten dealers could take a hike, and the sole survivor could stay open merely as a service station. Or you can skip past all the pain, give up the fight, and trade your dealership in for a quick lube.

It's a regular wild-west stagecoach holdup. Or perhaps like a terrifying scene from an H.G. Wells book where towering three-legged "fighting-machines" descend from the heavens and start shooting the place up.

These are the Profit Snatchers. And they're coming for you. Actually, many of them are already here, living in and among us, posing as your friends and "partners," speaking at conferences, writing in magazines, showing up at stores with donuts, glad handing and acting like they care. They don't.

But you already know that.

All this has been neatly disguised as "value pricing" or "one price" or "transparency" or "true." This slop is being peddled to unsuspecting dealers who know there must be a better way, who desperately want to sell more cars. Of course, this "value" approach doesn't really make any sense. Where's the profit supposed to come from? But doing something is better than doing nothing, right?

Dealers are being persuaded to believe the only way to sell cars these days is to offer a low price. Often, the lowest price. Dealers, generally speaking, believe the car business is about merchandising vehicles (taking pictures, displaying inventory, pricing competitively, buying low). Simply put, that is a lousy, lame and broken model that's being pushed on you by factory reps, auctions and techo-babble fools.

"But why oh why would they steer me wrong?"

Consider this: the factories and the auctions make money when you BUY cars from them. Not when you sell cars for a PROFIT. They believe that the lower your prices are, the more cars you'll sell. Who cares about your profit? Not them. Best-case scenario for them is for you to sell the cars at dead cost, and figure out how to make money some other way. The last thing they want is for your profit to stand in the way of a sale.

Consider this, too: the gear heads don't understand the business. But they want to poach the business for some easy money. The car business is a HUGE business, and the private equity firms that back these tech companies want a piece of your bounty. Nothing wrong with that. As long as they add value and help make your life better or easier or make the business run more smoothly. But they don't understand the business. They only understand that they (personally) really like to clip coupons and order value meals and buy cheap junk from big box retailers. So everyone else must like that, too. And in their lazy, uncreative and unimaginative binary world, they concoct a half-baked plan to "help" dealers fight with one another to have the lowest prices. Don't hold it against them. It's the best they could come up with. They didn't possibly imagine there were other ways to "help" dealers sell more cars without giving away the store.

Terrifyingly (ironically and comically, too) many dealers have decided to break rank and side with the Snatchers. They've been brainwashed, possessed, and are actually hastening the destruction of the business, including the eradication of their own dealership. There's only one force strong enough to compel someone to willingly act in a way that will bring about their own demise: fear.

Like the man who spent 127 hours caught under an 800-pound boulder at the bottom of a canyon. <u>He cut off his own arm, because there appeared to be no other option.</u> And in his case, there wasn't.

But what about your situation?

Understand...dropping your prices and sacrificing profit is no different than cutting off your arm. Most dealers only resort to such extreme measures after deciding there's no other way out. Never mind that the action they hope will save them only brings them closer to their own extinction. They feel trapped and they act instinctively out of fear. Like lemmings following one after another, dealers look around and see that everyone else is apparently cutting their prices, shrinking their margins and offering cars for near zero profit (hoping to make it up on the backend or in future service business). So they do it, too.

Do you believe there's no other way out? Or are you still hoping against hope that things will go back to being the way they were, that the Profit Snatchers will head back to their home planet?

Sorry to bear such bad news, but the Profit Snatchers are here to stay. And they're out for blood. Frankly, staying in the business of selling cars with all this going on is crazy. Stark-raving-padded-white-room-one-flew-over-the-cuckoo's-nest crazy.

So what about your options? Is cutting your prices (amputation) the only way out of this mess? Truth be told, there is another option. But it's not well suited for most ordinary dealers. In fact, a lot of dealers probably should just cut their prices and hang on to the life raft for as long as they can. Realistically, you can probably survive that way (certainly not thrive) for another ten or twenty years. And for you, that may be enough. Do your time and get out. Who knows what stored equity or blue sky will be left by then? Who knows whether or not there will be anything to pass on to your family? But maybe you can at least survive between now and then off the scraps left by the "below invoice" mooches and whatever profit the Snatchers deem appropriate for you to make in any given year. Hopefully nobody will come up with some new web site where dealers offer to pay customers to take the cars. As long as they don't do that you should be OK for a while.

What's that you say? You're not comfortable merely surviving for the next ten or twenty years? Wait, you actually think you deserve to make a profit? (Hysterical and sinister cackling erupts in the evil lair.)

"Hell no!" you say? You're willing to arm yourself and fight back against the profit snatching men from Mars? Good! Then know this: you are not alone. We're here standing right by your side and we're not alone either. We've created our own army, our own weapons and we've discovered the Snatchers' weakness. If you have the gumption, the strength and the desire to fight we can show you how to not just survive this battle but to come out better, stronger and richer than you could ever imagine. And not just financially rich(er), but personally rich(er) as well.

The invasion may be underway but the war is not over. Let the Profit Snatchers gobble up the weak, meek and lame, and let's get busy building a new *car dealership business* where dealers are the heroes, the business is fun and profit is naturally and abundantly earned by dealers who provide real value, not just low prices.

The future of the car business is yours to create. We, along with our vast network of like-minded dealers, are here to help you and support you and share our unique methods for transforming your business and building a profitable dealership that will sustain far into the future. Reading this book is the first step.

In this book you will discover:

- A little-known way to make the car business fun again
- A new, growing paradigm where car dealers are viewed as respected and influential members of their communities

- A simple way to differentiate your dealership so that price is no longer the chief concern of your customers
- A complete system for marketing yourself in a way that produces more profit from every sale, increases repeat business and improves customer satisfaction
- A source of highly desirable, highly profitable customers who are seeking your real value and are willing to pay more to buy from you
- How to make your message appeal to 35 times more prospects
- Ultimately, how to build a business and live a life that's ESP—Enjoyable, Simple & Prosperous.

CHAPTER 2:

REVOLUTION

We have a vision of a future where the car business is enjoyable, dealers are respected and low price isn't the only thing that matters. A future where people in the car business will think bigger about who they are and what they do for the world. A future where dealers are important. A future where dealers know what value they really provide and embrace their calling as problem solvers, as advisors. A future where dealers put the emphasis on the customer, not the car and their differentiation is based not on product and price but on process and personality, on caring and character. A future where people respect and revere dealers for their expertise, commitment to exceptional service, and dedication to the community in which they live and the people they serve.

Unfortunately, the stereotype of the cheesy, two-bit scoundrel car dealer is alive and well today, and the move away from that stereotype has largely been a move away from profit and independence. The Profit Snatchers' fix for this big problem is for dealers to work for next to nothing and to fight with one another for the so-called privilege of selling the cars for near cost.

But we believe good dealers deserve a better reputation than they have right now, wouldn't you agree? We believe good dealers don't deserve to be treated or categorized as criminals. We believe good dealers shouldn't be hated, feared and reviled as they are today. We believe good dealers, those who are advisors, problem solvers and who provide exceptional service, should be rewarded.

These words are guiding us to an important place and an important truth. The car business has never been tougher or more talked about. But we wonder if now, more than a century after the first Model T was produced, we haven't completely forsaken our purpose and our reason for being in this business. And too few dealers are standing up to the oppressors.

Our collective voice must speak up. These words must be heard right now because dealers are under attack—you are under attack. The battle is for dealer survival. Ominous threats loom everywhere. But your deadliest opponents are posing as your friends. There are forces within the automotive industry that are trying to commoditize dealers. These invaders are hell bent on diminishing the role of dealers, with a stated goal of making traditional dealerships obsolete. Their plan is for your dealership to be nothing more than a vehicle pickup location and a service center. Is that OK with you?

You may not notice this as the bloody and brutal battle that it actually is, but it is real and the casualties are mounting. The time to pick a side, to stand up and fight, is now, or it may be too late. If we continue too far down the current path there will be no going back. Right now the current of change is taking us in a dangerous direction, down the wrong path.

Like it or not, there is a collusion of power within the industry that is programming consumers to believe that "low price" is the only important factor to consider when buying a car. Simultaneously, these very same forces are trying to convince dealers that "low price" is the only effective way to differentiate one dealership from any other. Essentially, these colluding powers are attempting to level prices across the industry, diminishing your profit in the process. But who benefits from this bloody price war? Certainly not dealers, not you, and, frankly, not consumers either.

It's a vicious cycle. Robbing you of your profit is robbing you of your power, your potency, your liberty and your independence as an entrepreneur. As profit is systematically reduced, so, too is your ability to provide exceptional service, solve problems and be an advisor. Thin margins reduce you to a merchant, and nothing more, like someone running a stall at a flea market, haggling over used tools. And buying a car becomes akin to buying gas. A dreaded chore that customers hope to complete by spending as little money as possible.

The end result of this process is a future where:

- Dealers are unnecessary.
- Dealerships are glorified repair shops, places for merely looking, not buying.
- Buying is done online through a manufacturer's website or a large online vehicle clearinghouse.
- Where you are an order taker and servant rather than a leader.

The former glory of dealerships as a center of their communities will be a faded memory.

The time when dealers employed many local people, funded community events, were civic leaders and supported local charities will be a thing of the past.

The excitement of getting a car will be reduced to a private experience where the individual alone relishes in the enjoyment...but not over the car, over the price.

If these aligned powers have their way, dealers won't be allowed to make a profit for selling a car. All the cars will be priced the same and that price will include a razor thin margin, barely sufficient to pay someone to process the paperwork. But, of course, you'll have the hope of future service business.

Stripped away will be what everyone is currently overlooking: the actual service you provide. It's not selling cars. The car business used to be a people business but the Profit Snatchers are taking over and turning it into a transactional business of commodities. Like trading pork bellies, corn on a computer, or buying a book from amazon.com.

But what about the people who need help, have questions or are looking for advice? They will be lost in the vast sea of impersonal, impractical and unmanageable online information. The business dealers are really in is helping these people. Anyone can peddle commodities and take orders. Only good car dealers can help people and really solve problems that are keeping them from getting the car they want or need.

The relentless attempt to program consumers to believe the car business revolves solely around price will be a fatal blow against tired and weary dealers who lack the strength, energy or zeal to fight back.

The Profit Snatchers demand obedience and subordination from dealers, insisting that front-end profit is a thing of the past and that today's dealers need to realize that less (profit) is more. Dealers are being corralled into a crowded elevator that's headed for the bottom floor: commoditization.

In the process, dealers are losing the battle with all that is personal and real about our business. What used to be a people business is now a technology business. What used to be enjoyable is now dreaded. What used to be an asset is now a liability. Can you remember a time when the car business was fun?

This likely future is a nightmare scenario that dealers should be fighting to avoid. You can choose to join the fight against these Snatchers...the fight for INDEPENDENCE...or you can assimilate...**be slowly homogenized, commoditized, equalized, and finally downsized.**

We are now at the point of transformation in this industry. A crossroads. But this isn't something to fear. We come to you not only with a challenge, but with answers too.

A BRIGHTER FUTURE

We believe there is another version of the future where the seemingly inevitable misery and impotence of dealers is avoided. It is a future where the car business is fun and profitable again. It's the renaissance of a once glorious business.

In truth, it's a revolution. And you are needed.

Here's our position:

- The car business should be enjoyable...even fun, again.
- Car dealers should be respected and influential members of their communities.
- Dealerships should have a competitive advantage other than low price.

Some might call this a personal manifesto. But we think of this more as a mission statement for the entire car dealer industry. We're proposing a better kind of success and we can get there together. In fact, we've already helped hundreds of dealers fight back and reclaim their passion and their profit.

Here's how to begin:

First, pick a side. You must choose or it will be chosen for you. You can take a passive role and let the future happen to you or you can take an active role and fight for what's rightfully yours to create...the future you desire.

You are welcome to share our vision for the future. We're glad for you to join us and the hundreds of other dealers who have already chosen fun, respect, profit and prosperity as their future. If these words echo strongly your own private thoughts then you've already made up your mind. Join in the fight against the Profit Snatchers.

Second, quit the price war. Pull the troops out. Throw up the white flag. The cost of victory is complete destruction and annihilation of the car business as we know it.

Third, declare that there is something unique about you and your dealership...a reason for customers to choose to do business with you over other dealers, other than low price. Even if you can't enunciate what that difference is right now, don't worry. We can help.

Fourth, commit to this new set of values:

❶ **The Car Business Should Be Fun:** Americans have a love affair with cars. Cars are an extension of our personalities. Our neighbors and co-workers see the car we drive and judge us by it. The powerful force of the human ego is intertwined with every American's desire for a nicer, newer car. You can use that desire as a force of positivity and prosperity. You can help people get the nicer, newer car they so ardently desire and make a very healthy profit in the process. It's fun to help people get what they want.

❷ **Car Dealers Should Be Respected:** Merchants ensnared in a price war aren't respected. They're walked on. By exiting the price war and committing to providing exceptional service and being a problem solver for your customers you can regain the confidence of your community. By positioning yourself as a force of help in your community and by actually offering support, you can rise again to be a beacon of respect.

❸ **Dealerships Should Not Compete On Price:** Study after study of consumer buying behavior has found that price ranks low on the list of reasons buyers buy. Participating in the price war erodes the confidence and respect customers have in you. There are huge masses of prospects available to you who are yearning for something other than the lowest price. But they're invisible to you and you're invisible to them as long as you continue to be a pawn in the Snatchers' commodity game. Instead of fighting to offer the lowest price, you can increase the value of the service you provide and have all the customers you can handle.

Why is this so important? Well, did you dream of more than this for your business? For your life? When did this become acceptable? Is this why you signed up to be a dealer? Or are you still in business to make a profit? And do you believe that the profit you make should be determined by how much value you bring to the marketplace? Or should YOUR PROFIT be dictated by a piece of software or a suit in a corporate office somewhere?

Privately, dealers and managers are fathers, mothers, sons, daughters, parishioners, mentors, counselors, friends, leaders and contributors. You play important roles in the lives of others. You help people get the transportation they so badly desire and need. In a depressed world you make people happy. But until you dedicate yourself to worthier goals than selling a car for the lowest price, you're on a mission of emptiness.

Here are important questions to consider:

- What do you stand for?

- What will you be remembered for?
- Are you a person or just a slave to the Profit Snatchers?

Let's bring back the soul and character to the future that is here today. We're calling for dealers to reconsider and recreate what they're all about. To reclaim the original glimmer of passion that got them here in the first place.

This is a revolution! A movement that's not just about features and benefits or cars and prices. An insurrection of value against the destroyers, the looters and moochers.

The beauty of this plan is that it only requires a slight adjustment. A change in perspective. A change in how we look at ourselves and the role we play in this business, in this world.

If you take this seriously and want to change the future for your business, we can arm you with the battle gear that will help you thrive. This book can help you take a completely different path. The ideas we're going to share with you have been the secret weapon in the war against commoditization for some of the most profitable dealers of our time.

If you know that our mission is your mission, if you are on our side in this battle for the future as a prosperous place for dealers, then you need a battle plan.

In your market, right now, there's a hotbed of buyers who haven't been brainwashed by the Snatchers. In fact, there are more of them than there are of the others. But you need to be able to find them and communicate with them in a compelling way.

We'll show you how to identify those highly desirable, highly profitable customers who are seeking your real value and the service you provide. You'll be able to determine:

- The size of your hidden opportunity
- Who they are and how you can reach them
- What they want to hear and receive from you

Armed with this information, you'll be prepared to revolt against the Profit Snatchers and start charting your own course toward a business that's what we call ESP—Enjoyable, Simple & Prosperous.

CHAPTER 3:

THE LOW PRICE DELUSION

Lower prices + lower profits = more cars sold.

So this is the formula for success in the car business today, huh? WOW! That's innovative, that's creative, that's ground breaking...YEAH RIGHT. There are some pretty major flaws in this formula. We'll investigate the flaws in a moment, but first let's explore the basis of this "success" formula a bit deeper. This is where the rodeo gets interesting.

So the Snatchers' pitch is that if you reduce your prices (they call this transparency—but it's not, it's stupidity), you'll sell more cars and ultimately make more money. The myth is based on the flawed logic that if you sell for less you'll naturally make up the difference in volume because of all the new customers you'll attract by having the lowest price on the vehicle each and every person is looking for.

Just for the record, there is a real corporate business strategy that is based on losing money on every single transaction, but volume doesn't help you much and it's not the end game of this strategic play. The battle plan for that game is to sustain the loss long enough to drive all competition out of your space. But that's an incredibly risky, play-for-keeps kind of game and it's a game that can't ever be won in the car business by any single point dealer.

For most dealers there will always be competition in the car business and the harsh reality is that there will always be someone willing to sell a car cheaper than you.

The Snatchers' poisonous prescription for success also fails to take into consideration this little gem: There is no second lowest.

You either have the lowest price or you do not have the lowest price. There's no second place finish in the race to the bottom.

But ultimately the biggest problem with the low price and volume formula is that it doesn't actually work. Your volume will only naturally increase if you are truly the absolute lowest priced guy on the block. But most dealers typically have way too much overhead to ever be that guy. Our members all have brick-and-mortar stores, staff, inventory costs, real estate expenses, floor plan expenses, customer service costs, legal fees, etc., all the things that go into running a real operation. If that's also the case for you, we've got bad news for you...you'll never be the lowest priced dealer. Or you won't be for very long. You'll be out of business in no time, abducted by the Snatchers. Why? Because there will always be a smaller guy with less overhead, less serious about the business and less caring about his customers who will ultimately price cars lower because he can. And if there's no little guy in your market, then there's probably a mega dealer nearby who can leverage economies of scale to out price you. That puts you in the place of second lowest or worse, somewhere above that, playing a game that can only be won by having the lowest price.

Once you are no longer the absolutely lowest priced opportunity, people are no longer basing their decision to buy from you solely on price considerations. Once you move away from strictly price-based selling, you enter the realm of value, service, positioning, location, marketing and a whole list of other factors that influence the buying decision. These factors are all controllable, scalable and able to be manipulated by you, which can allow you to generate prospects and sell cars without having the lowest price. In fact, you can have the highest prices and if you are good at leveraging these other buying factors and differentiators you can sell more cars and make lots of profit in the process. We help dealers do it everyday.

The Snatchers don't want you to know this, but once you are no longer the lowest priced option, you are forced in to the game of differentiation using criteria other than price. So, the traffic will not increase naturally, automatically giving you additional volume like they said it would. So you either get abducted (go out of business) or you will eventually be forced to do something different. Essentially, you'll be back where you started only financially a lot poorer and personally worn out from their intense, full-body, all-cavity experimentation.

To save yourself, you must start focusing, working and spending money on improving these other buying criteria that impact the way people choose the dealership they decided to do business with and what they deem a fair price to actually be. This is what we call...providing real VALUE.

There is a huge difference between providing real value and giving someone the lowest price. Many so-called "experts" believe they are synonymous but they are not even in the same ballpark. Value is made up of the factors like trust, ease, professionalism, services, solutions, personality, character, experience, environment, expertise, positioning, celebrity and many other very subtle factors we haven't even touched on and probably won't in this book.

Once a prospect moves from strictly price-based decision making and enters a value-based decision making process the competitive advantage of price goes out the window and your chances of making profit based on naturally increasing volume due to low price disappears in the blink of an eye.

Lowest price is actually a gimmick created by the Snatchers to ensnare dealers who don't know how to or don't think they have the time to do the work it truly takes to provide value and differentiate themselves. They lure dealers into financing their own demise by giving them a carrot that is irresistibly attractive and seemingly solves all their problems and takes the "ugliness" and "salesiness" out of the business. A promise of pure harmony and bliss, like the lure of a Marxist society with all the glamour and all the results of one, as well. On the surface this all seem great. Everyone seems to love the idea. Problem is, nobody really loves being broke.

So if you've realized that the Snatchers' success secret is actually Satan's spawn and you believe that providing real value for money is the true way to creating a business and life that are ESP—Enjoyable, Simple and Prosperous, then you're probably asking yourself the question, "How do I do it?"

Now that's the million-dollar question (or in our members' cases, the multimillion-dollar question), isn't it?

CHAPTER 4:

TRUST US

I n the pages that follow, you'll discover how to break free from the Profit Snatchers' grip, multiply your market and tap into a pool of highly profitable prospects that's 35 times larger than the population you're selling to right now. We're going to show you how to make your advertising and marketing dramatically more effective by including three simple elements, which you're most likely leaving out completely right now. We'll show you how to position yourself comfortably in a category of one, which will make you the only and obvious choice in your market. You'll learn how to answer the two questions everybody in North America is silently asking themselves, which must be answered before they buy a car. Ultimately, you'll discover the secret weapon you can use to defeat the Profit Snatchers and start enjoying prosperity in life and business once again.

But first, you should be asking, "Who are you guys?" and "Why do you have the answers?" and "Why should I trust you?"

For starters, every two minutes a dealer sells a car using our strategies. In total, we've helped dealers sell well over two million vehicles, and the number continues climbing every day. We've directly generated over $12 billion in sales and dealers have spent over $100 million advertising with our approach. We've created dramatic results for dealers selling Chevy, Ford, Dodge, Chrysler, Kia, Hyundai, Mazda, Suzuki, Mitsubishi, Honda, Toyota, Nissan...even Mercedes-Benz. We've had a lot of practice.

We've been recognized for our accomplishments in publications like *Entrepreneur Magazine, Investors Business Daily, Businessweek, Brandweek, Advertising Age, Direct Marketing News, Forbes, Inc. Magazine*...even *Ripley's Believe it or Not*.

As the authors of *Gravitational Marketing: The Science of Attracting Customers*, a bestselling book in bookstores nationwide and around the world, and the founders of Rich Dealers International, we are experts who provide usable, practical and realistic advice. <u>More importantly, we only share ideas that we've proven to be effective.</u>

It's something that we insist on because we know your time is valuable, as is ours. We've all got other things we could be doing besides writing or reading another book. We want this to be a huge return on investment for you.

Now, what you should realize about us is that the cars we've helped sell haven't been sold at the lowest price or with slim margins. In fact, our members don't talk about prices in their advertising, yet they consistently outsell their competitors and do it all while working less and enjoying life more.

So how do we do all this?

We use Gravitational Marketing, of course, which is a pretty powerful idea that has been used by thousands of businesses across six continents.

We've been invited to speak to audiences around the world. Our books have been published in many languages and ideas implemented, effectively, around the world. Business owners from more than one hundred industries have invested their time and money to learn our techniques. Lucky for you, our passion is the car business. And our home court is the USA. There's no better business and no better country in which to leverage the powerful methods you'll discover here.

We've been personally influenced by powerful people whose names you surely know. George Forman (the grill guy), Gene Simmons (the tongue guy), Billy Mays (the OxyClean guy), Elizabeth Dole (the senator), George Ross (the Donald's right hand man), Robert Cialdini (the master of persuasion), Warren Buffet (the billionaire). These are all people we've sought out for their unique wisdom and experiences. From them we've discovered that most people think "too small" and worry "too big."

In 2004, after a meeting about small business and entrepreneurship with then-Governor Jeb Bush and realizing what a bigger-than-life personality he was, we became committed to breaking free of the small-minded thinking that afflicts so many businesses and to share that "big" idea with as many people as possible.

Sure, there are plenty of ways to make money in business. Certainly easier roads than the path we've chosen. But we've chosen to be mavericks, gunslingers...straight shooters. We promised each other that we would "tell it like it is" and since then we've earned a reputation as "harsh reality" types with likeable personalities. Most importantly, we've earned the respect and trust of hundreds of dealers we've personally helped achieve incredible success.

All this is meant to explain to you that we know what we're talking about, have pure intentions and deserve your trust, respect and attention.

Before we go any further into the "how to" advice, there's something else you need to know about us and about our approach.

It's something we call ESP. We're not talking about mind reading, no. In our world, ESP stands for "Enjoyable, Simple & Prosperous!" We live our lives and we run our business in a way that's Enjoyable, Simple & Prosperous, and we teach dealers how to make their businesses and lives Enjoyable, Simple & Prosperous, too. How's that for a goal? Selling cars and making money is neat. But the sales and cash don't matter one iota if you're not enjoying a life of simplicity and prosperity. Can we all agree on that?

This brings some heavy implications. For instance, we won't recommend strategies that will make your life miserable. We firmly believe that life shouldn't suck. Even the car business! Sometimes a method or tactic we show you won't lead to the quickest buck or the easiest sale. But instead our ideas are sustainable, doable, repeatable and scalable. We flatly refuse to rely on gimmicks and hype. Why bother with that when there's a simple way to sell all the cars you could ever want to sell—and enjoy life in the process?

Ultimately, it's a realization of the fact that there's far more to life than just selling more cars and making money. That's the easy part of the car business. We'll show you how to sell more cars and make more money, no problem. The more challenging part is how to do that and live a better life simultaneously.

How do you live a more fulfilled life doing the things you love to do with the people you love to do them with? That is what makes up the fabric of a quality life experience, and that's what we believe a business should be about: delivering a quality life experience to you, not having a business that makes you a slave to Profit Snatchers.

ESP isn't just for you either. It starts with you, as a belief, an ideal. Then it spreads to your managers and your staff. Soon, you'll find yourself talking about ESP to your family, friends and customers. Our mission is to make life and business Enjoyable, Simple & Prosperous for as many people as possible. Each time another dealership leverages our ideas, ESP touches more people. What an amazing side-effect of selling cars!

THIS ONE TIME, AT BAND CAMP

Before we were marketing wizards, we were just a couple of broke guys in college who met on the marching band field in Orlando, Florida in August of 1995. Seriously.

We became fast friends, and here we are together, all these years later, creating incredible results for dealers (and other businesses) around the world.

But when we met, we had a problem. Travis was on the road to becoming an engineer and Jim was on the path to becoming an optometrist. It wasn't going too well.

The problem was we were being forced to endure Calculus, which is really round-peg-through-square-hole kind of stuff for a couple of creative guys, and the result was that we both flunked the class. Obviously, with a big F on the report card, we weren't going to get very far in a science profession.

That left us with very few options, which forced us into the great field of marketing and advertising. That's how we ended up doing this. It was a fateful and fortuitous occurrence.

It was an event that changed the course of our personal history, and has also now had a ripple effect that's changed the course of many business-owners, entrepreneurs, and car dealers, lives in the process. Conservatively, millions of lives have been positively touched by what we do. What's allowed us to make such a dramatic impact is the one-two punch of Gravitational Marketing and our ESP philosophy.

The genesis of Gravitational Marketing came from a discovery we made in the storage closet at our first job after college. We were both working at an automotive advertising agency. We happened upon this closet, and inside the closet were bags, garbage bags, filled with something very bizarre. What we did with that strange something most people would consider a form of cruel and unusual punishment.

SEEK AND YE SHALL FIND

We've always believed in the power of seeking solutions. Throughout our lives, each of us has found, time and time again, that the solution to just about any problem lies just beyond the reach of ordinary, lazy people. Winners know that solutions are hiding in plain sight, ready for the taking, waiting for a bold seeker of solutions to come along. Losers suffer lives of mediocrity simply because they can't be bothered to look around the corner for an alternative. If life hands you lemons, most people accept them (some attempt lemonade). We hand the lemons back and ask for apples, please and thank you. Most people are content "getting what they get"—we aren't, and you shouldn't be, either. Don't like your situation? Change something, seek something different.

The reason we were looking in that closet in the first place was because we had been tasked with an impossible mission: come up with a way to sell the worst selling cars in America, which at the time happened to be Kias. Yikes!

They said, "Guys, can you come up with a program? Can you come up with a way to fix this?" Not many other people in the agency wanted to work with these clients and, being the new guys, we didn't know exactly where to start.

But we attacked this problem with ferocity and intensity. We didn't see failure as an option. We set out on a life or death mission of elevating these clients from failure to success and prosperity.

So we decided to go back in history and find out what had worked before. We created a radical plan to develop a formula by analyzing the pattern of past successes and then applying it to that list of clients they gave us.

A DIRTY DISCOVERY

Frustratingly, we were getting nowhere fast. Then one day, almost as if created by our own tenacious and unbending belief that a solution did exist, this closet (which, by the way, we had never really noticed before) appeared. We opened the door and saw the bags. When we opened up the bags, guess what we found inside?

The bags were stuffed with cassette tapes and videotapes, an odd discovery for most, but we were thrilled. These tapes were recordings of the automotive commercials from dealership clients of the agency from the previous 13 years. After doing a bit of research, we found that these tapes used to be categorized alphabetically and hung on a wall, for reference purposes or maybe just for display purposes. Now, after a move, they had gotten lost in the shuffle and ended up in trash bags, forgotten in a closet.

Here's where the magic happened. We started listening to these tapes. One man's trash is another man's treasure, right? In this case, it was absolutely true. We started listening to these recordings and researching which clients' advertising campaigns produced the greatest results.

We may not have fared well in calculus, but we both have always had an unbending commitment to creatively solving problems. We always find a solution. In this case, the solution came from carefully analyzing our discovery. We found the clients that sold the most cars and made the most money, and who were subsequently clients for the longest time with the agency. We used the sales logs to cross-reference the ads they ran—and had success with—and looked for common traits among these ads, searching for patterns to emerge.

It's very similar to Napoleon Hill's work with the book *Think and Grow Rich*. Hill analyzed the top 500 wealthiest people in the world and then came back and figured out what their commonalities were, distilling those commonalities into success principles.

Through our research and analysis, we discovered which commercials were the most successful and separated the wheat from the chaff, the good from the bad, and uncovered the commonalities among the best. This little discovery became the seed that's blossomed into Gravitational Marketing today.

The fundamental principles of what made those commercials successful became the secret ingredients of our recipe for rapid success. We may as well have unlocked the secret to cold fusion! We emerged from that closet as superheroes. Armed and dangerous, we started transforming the way car dealers advertised.

Using our rare and super-charged powers of problem solving and creativity, we set out to change the world, one customer at a time. The results were unimaginably powerful. That dirty discovery started a chain-reaction that continues to drive sales and profit today, 13 years later.

THE PRESENT REALITY

It's good that right now you're considering a different approach at your store. Now you're taking advice from two guys who've done it and who've got a formula that can be shared with you...a formula that has been proven to work and that you will benefit from.

Obviously we've come a long way since the tapes in the garbage bags. We've done a lot of testing and measuring, spent over $100 million in advertising, implementing Gravitational Marketing all over the world. After humble beginnings, it's grown into quite an enormous machine that generates astounding results.

In fact, as we were writing this, an email came across the private discussion group our members use to support each other and share ideas. It was from a Chevy dealer in Indiana. The email said:

"Wow! We have been a member since October 2010 and the numbers just keep getting BIGGER AND BIGGER!! We've TAKEN so much great information from this group. Love the meetings and the books...they seem to accelerate growth!

"This month is an ALL TIME FEBRUARY RECORD & VERY CLOSE to an ALL TIME RECORD! 428 UNITS. Gross per unit, $3,000 plus. That will work! We themed this year as the 12 records of 2012! So far we are two months into it and 2 for 2! Hope everyone closes VERY STRONG & gets off to an awesome start in March. Let's Do It!!"

This is not unusual. In fact, messages like these come through the group every week. This message, and the hundreds of others like it, prove why you should trust us and join forces with us. There's a way to beat the Profit Snatchers, and it's not overly complicated. You can do it, too.

Next we're going to share with you the formula that has made the machine work so well and secrets that will help you overcome the problems you are facing in your store today. We'll layout the battle plan for defeating the Profit Snatchers.

CHAPTER 5:

TRAFFIC FIXES EVERYTHING

Without a doubt, the car business has struggled in recent years, but there's a perfectly reasonable explanation. Now, it's important to understand that we're not talking about the car business in general and everything that makes up the car business, including the manufacturers, the after-market, and all the different fingered components that connect together to make up the entire industry.

What we are talking about is you, the retail car dealership. Whether you are a franchise or an independent dealer doesn't matter to us; you're on the hook buying cars and selling cars every day, and that is what we are talking about. This message applies to you.

There's a set of problems you're facing right now. Many of those problems are caused by the wicked will of the Profit Snatchers. They're fogging dealers' brains and creating an alternate customer reality where price is the only thing that matters. But the good news is we have the antidote to their mind-altering poison. By identifying the problems we can overcome them and start to unlock the secret to selling more cars right now without promising the lowest price.

Once you admit that you have a problem you can seek out a solution. If you have less traffic and fewer opportunities than you used to, and if you're selling fewer cars than you need to be or ought to be, that's a problem. There's no good reason to settle for less than you want, less than you need or less than you deserve. Even if you've gotten used to selling fewer cars and even if you've grown accustomed to having less traffic, that doesn't mean it has to continue that way. Don't settle for mediocrity when greatness lies right around the corner. Face it, you need to sell more cars and get more traffic. Every dealer does!

Another problem could be that grosses are down and all your customers seem to be price shoppers. That's a huge problem! Being engaged in a price war sucks. It's a zero sum battle that promises to leave no winners in the end. Think nuclear armageddon. Only the cockroaches survive (we'll leave you to determine who the cockroaches are).

Many dealers tell us their problem is that the business just isn't fun anymore. They feel that they've lost interest, excitement and enthusiasm for the business, and now it's just a grind. The result is a miserable existence that weighs heavily on your personal sanity and on your family life.

Of course there's a million other problems you may have: not enough new car inventory, overpriced used cars, floor plan issues, partner problems, poor management, thickheaded dealer, expiring leases or manufacturer shenanigans. But here's an interesting idea: if you had all the traffic you could handle, could you find a way to fix all of those other problems?

Sure you could. A landslide of customers allows you to stop fighting over price. That means you can sell the cars for more, which means you can buy the cars for more. That instantly fixes inventory supply issues. You can buy all the cars you ever need, and more, if you give up trying to buy them at the lowest price (funny how this low price thing always seems to bite you in the ass). Problems with partners tend to dissipate in the wake of huge traffic surges because the money starts flowing and everyone settles down. The banks really like it when the cash starts flowing, too. So if you manage the details properly, floor plan issues can vanish. Typically the factory reps become your best friend once sales become brisk. And the extra cash flow will help you fix a host of other bothersome maladies. A lot of traffic gives you tremendous power in attracting the top management and sales talent. Even stubborn absentee dealers (if you happen to be stuck with one of those) lighten up when they see the numbers jump up significantly. You see, increasing traffic truly has the power to fix everything.

We're not saying this is easy. It's not. You and your team will have to be fast and furious to keep up. And you sure as hell better know the nuts and bolts of the car business cold. But it's fun and exciting. And what a relief it is to go from slow sales to a bunch of low price mooches to fast sales to happy customers who let you make a profit and beg you to help them.

One of the things you're really going to love about our approach is that it can make you so much money by helping you sell so many more cars while living such a better lifestyle at the same time. Many dealers tell us that our approach makes the car business fun again.

In fact, just recently a Hyundai dealer in the Northeast announced to the group that she had wrapped up a record month, with 173 sales in one store versus 102 the same month, prior year, and 109 at her other store versus 62 the same month, prior year. But the most important part of her message was about how she was actually having fun in the process and truly enjoying the car business again. We hear it time and again from our members that a business they grew to hate is now fun and exciting again, not to mention extremely profitable.

It's really a magical combination. Isn't it good to be able to sell more and work less? The answer is obviously, yes, of course it is, and it's the goal that every dealer should have in mind when they approach this business.

That's what this is all about.

Next we're going to show you the big roadblocks, the big reasons why you're getting less traffic and selling fewer cars and how to turn that around, fast. We think of these as "Rumble Strips"—you know, those ridges in the road that are designed to slow down traffic?

CHAPTER 6:

THE HIDDEN MARKET

Let's take a look at the first reason that traffic is down so dramatically: the market has been slashed. Everyone knows that there are far fewer buyers in the market today than there were in the past. This is an obvious reality in the car business today.

Doesn't that suck?

There are simply fewer buyers out there than there were previously. This is the explanation behind why so many dealerships saw their sales cut in half. Most dealers in any area are fighting with one another for "their fair share" of the market. All this talk about market share and market penetration causes dealers to view the car buyer universe as a limited pool. It's believed that there are a finite number of sales that will happen in the market in any given period of time. So in order for one dealer to sell more, necessarily, another dealer must sell less. It's a big tug-of-war between all the dealers in the market.

Naturally, of course, cutting prices seems like a smart way to compete. Especially when everyone else is doing it. This is the Profit Snatchers' brainwash in action. This is exactly what they want you to believe and exactly how they want you to behave. Their exploitation of the market is already taking hold and it allows them to manipulate some dealers' decision-making and actions like a puppeteer manipulates his puppet.

However, our 27 years of combined experience working with over 500 dealers and helping sell more than two million cars has proven that the car buyer universe is not nearly as limited as most believe. It would be a stretch to call it infinite, but let's call it vast. Interestingly, a large percentage of the more than two million cars we've helped sell have been incremental sales that didn't come at the expense of other dealers. Literally, it is possible to create sales out of thin air, selling to customers who weren't planning to buy a car. Let us explain...

If you analyze the overall market, you'll find that roughly two percent of the people in any geographic area are currently shopping for a nicer, newer vehicle, be it new or used. That means that a whopping 98 percent of people in the area are not shopping at all.

This percentage has decreased in recent years because of fear, recessionary worries, low consumer confidence, economic instability, political unrest, inventory problems, gas prices, and credit problems resulting in the decreased ability to get financing. Even the real estate crisis has had a big impact. Unemployment and even the bad news of unemployment splashed across the evening news night after night has had an impact. But these are all factors that we cannot control.

In the meantime, most dealers are fighting over that two percent of in-market buyers (we call these people intenders). And nearly everyone is completely ignoring the 98 percent (we call these people non-intenders). Seems to make sense, doesn't it? Why bother paying attention to people who aren't shopping? Some people yap about creating brand awareness or top of mind presence. That's a cute idea, but it doesn't actually work, and dealers aren't willing to spend money on that. So the 98 percent, the non-intenders, go ignored.

All the while, the intenders stay up late at night stalking dealers' web sites, doing research, trying to determine how best to steal the car from the "greedy" car dealer. They find web sites that purport to expose the "true" price a dealer paid for the car. Of course, that's about what they're willing to pay.

Let the games begin! This person becomes a lead by entering their information into multiple dealers' web sites and multiple third party vehicle listing services, and next thing you know, the tug-of-war is raging! Dealers are fighting for this customer and the handful of others that have entered the market that day.

At the end of the month, the in-market intenders have been scattered all around the map, with each dealer selling a little more or a little less than the average. Everyone is exhausted, there's blood on the floor, you've won some, you've lost some. But you never seem to make any major strides. That's because you're fighting over scraps, when you could be hording the tenderloin and the chops all for yourself.

The biggest opportunity in the car business is learning to market to and attract the non-intenders, the 98 percent. These are people who haven't done much research, don't know (or care) what you paid for the car. These are people who are excited to get a nicer, newer car, and are willing and eager buyers, as long as you can help them get what they want.

THE 98 PERCENT CHALLENGE

For a moment, think about your own house and ask yourself whether you own a washing machine and a dryer. Most people do. Most people tell us that they can remember when they got their washer or dryer. It was either there when they moved into the house, or purchased when their old washer or dryer broke down. Usually there's an event that causes people to invest in a new washer or dryer. Most people aren't out just fun shopping for new washing machines or dryers. Most people, probably about 98 percent of people, aren't shopping for a new washing machine or dryer at all right now.

Under the presumption that you are not shopping for a new washing machine or dryer, if you were to open the paper this Sunday, and a Sears ad were to fall out with pictures of appliances on it full of special offers ($0 down!) and sale prices and discounts ($399 off!), would you pay any attention? What if another ad from Lowes or Home Depot were to fall out, touting zero percent financing, with a huge selection and free delivery? Would that capture your attention? What if you saw an ad on a web site offering 25% off all appliances and promising outstanding customer service?

Would you care one bit about any of this? Of course not, because you're not shopping; it's all meaningless. You're not in the market for appliances. An advertiser could offer the lowest prices in the world, free delivery, zero percent financing, tiny monthly payments, no money down and it'd be meaningless to you.

Now if you compare this type of advertising to typical automotive advertising you would find them to be strikingly similar, almost identical. Obviously one has cars and one has appliances, but they've got the same basic elements: offers and prices—a typical retail-oriented ad.

Now, just like in the car business, there's two percent shopping and 98 percent not shopping, which means this ad, any of these ads, fall on deaf ears with 98 percent of the people in the marketplace. A full 98 percent of the

<u>people never see these ads, never pay any attention.</u> What does this mean?

It's a waste! Do the media outlets offer a 98 percent discount since 98 percent of the audience is ignoring the ad? Of course not. So it's money down the drain.

Now, think for a moment about your advertising and about the advertising of other car dealerships in your area and ask yourself, does it feature vehicles? Does it show price and payments? Does it talk service? Does it talk about selection? Does it have offers related to the down payment? While those might all be important components of a good retail ad, you realize now that just as you wouldn't pay attention to the washing machine and dryer ads, 98 percent of the people in your market are not paying attention to your ads. They're not paying attention to the advertising that they hear or see or come into contact with that's talking about vehicles and prices and payments and down payments, because they're not shopping! Retail-oriented advertising will never attract the 98 percent.

On top of that, think about what's happening on the Internet these days. There's this huge push to merchandise vehicles online. But are people who aren't shopping for cars ever going to visit an online vehicle-listing service? Absolutely not. They wouldn't dream of it! So listing vehicles at low prices online doesn't attract the 98 percent either.

What's a dealer to do?

THE 98 PERCENT SOLUTION

If you were in the appliance business you'd be in trouble. Thankfully, you're in the car business and things are a lot different.

Here's what you need to understand. In the car business, there's a way to turn the 98 percent, the non-intenders, the non-shoppers, into buyers. The reason is that people care about their vehicles. They care about the car they drive, more than they care about washers and dryers and most other products. The love of the automobile is engrained in the fabric of what it means to be an American. Cars are a part of American culture, a part of our identities. Our neighbors see us driving our car, our co-workers see us pull up in our car, our friends and family ride in our car, and the car that sits in our driveway represents our family. The car is a status symbol. Our car represents who we are and how we feel about ourselves. These things are important.

If people drove to work in their washing machine or dryer, they'd care a lot more about what kind of washer and dryer they owned. And we'd be working our magic in the appliance business.

Generally, people wait for the washer and dryer to break down completely before buying a new one. But thankfully, people change vehicles long before their old car breaks down completely (otherwise there'd be no used car market). That's a huge difference between appliances (and lots of other items for sale) and cars.

The realization here is that, although only two percent of people are actively shopping for a car at any given time, **at all times everybody wants a nicer, newer car.**

Imagine for a moment how good it would feel if everybody in the market was your potential customer.

Most dealers are simply waiting to get their fair share of the in-market customers and saying, "I can't control how many people are shopping for cars. All I can do is offer competitive prices, try to provide good service and hopefully get my fair share of the people who're in the market," and the bad news is there is absolutely no growth potential in that way of thinking because it truly is out of your control. If the market gets better, if more cars start being sold, you'll probably sell more cars too (great business model). But outside of extraordinary exceptions, it's almost impossible to get an inordinately greater share of the in-market buyers. If you want to sell more cars right now, you have to take matters into your own hands. You have to create a paradigm shift, a market shift, and start drawing customers from the 98 percent.

To make matters worse, dealers are competing with each other for the in-market buyers based on price. Retail-oriented advertising and marketing is driven by low prices and big sales. It's a race to see who can spend the most money in advertising to sell cars for as little as possible.

Who really wins when you sell more cars but you sell them at a lower profit than the guy down the street? Do you win? Does the customer win? Actually, everyone loses. So our goal here is not just to sell more cars. The goal is to sell more cars without sacrificing our gross profit and let's not do it by just waiting for the market to get better. Let's sell more cars starting immediately and broaden our market to a much wider group of people so that our opportunity is bigger than every other dealer in the marketplace.

"If everybody wants a nicer, newer car, why isn't everybody shopping?"

There are two big reasons.

The first reason they aren't shopping is because they've taken themselves out of the market because they believe they have a credit issue that will keep them from getting approved for a loan. Maybe they've had a short sale or a period of unemployment. Maybe they've tried to get approved in the past and have been turned down or they've just been reading the paper, watching the news, talking to their friends and, based on their own situation and their viewpoint of the economic situation at the time, they do not feel it can happen for them, even if they want it to. And since their car isn't broken and they don't think they can get approved for another one, they are not going to set themselves up to be disappointed and face ridicule. They're out of the game, mentally, and, because they've taken themselves out mentally, they don't even see your ads. They completely ignore them, in the same way you ignore the washer and dryer ads. The sad truth is, you could probably help many of these people get a car if you only had the chance.

The second reason customers are out of the market is because of a trade issue. They already have a car and they're either making payments on that car, or they may believe they owe more on the car than it's worth. Most important, they believe they cannot get out of that car. Most people inaccurately assume they have to pay off their current lease or loan before getting another car. Obviously that's a false assumption. Can you imagine if people thought that way about their homes?

So millions of people have taken themselves out of the market, unnecessarily, without any kind of real information to back up their decision. People take themselves erroneously out of the market and then we treat them that way; we don't even give ourselves a chance to motivate them, to get them into our dealerships and to help them buy a car.

Because the vast majority of people with credit problems and trade issues aren't shopping, we know they aren't paying attention to ads with cars, prices and payments. In effect, you are invisible to them, but we also know that they would like a nicer, newer car, so the big opportunity lies in marketing to those out-of-market non-intenders, to the people who woke up this morning with no intention of buying a vehicle. The opportunity is in causing those people to pay attention, to act, to come in today, because there are an almost unlimited number of those people out there, and most dealerships are not communicating with them at all. And you can relax. You don't have to be worried about how to do this, because we've got a proven method for making it happen, which we will show you.

Ultimately, it's just not the right time for most people. It's your job to make it the right time. The good news is it's easier (and more profitable) to do that than it is to compete over price with all the other dealers just to win your little sliver of the intender market.

One of our members, for example, a Kia dealer from Pennsylvania, has actually completely exited the price war. In fact, if a price-seeking customer comes into his store, he asks them to leave. He'll give them directions to the store across town that sells cars at invoice. He's realized it's better for him if his competition gets that customer. In the meantime, he's gone from selling 80 cars a month to over 300 cars a month. None of those 300 sales are made on price. All of his customers are brought into the market by his advertising, and brought directly to his dealership, bypassing all other dealerships. By choosing to do business this way, his store runs better, his processes are smoother, his staff is happier and his customers love him.

It's okay not to believe us on this, but doing so would be a huge mistake on your part. There is near infinite power in everything that we've just explained. In fact, this is how you can begin fighting the Profit Snatchers and regaining your own independence.

CHAPTER 7:

THE SECRET TO STANDING OUT

93

The second big problem facing dealers today is that all dealers, all dealerships, look the same. We aren't talking about their physical look, although that too, but we're really talking about the public perception. The public is bombarded with automotive marketing messages that all look and sound the same. The sooner you realize the severity of this problem, the sooner you'll begin to reap the rewards of finding a solution to it.

Here's the reality: <u>Same Is Lame</u>. That's one of the big mantras among our members and a big overarching tenet of Gravitational Marketing. If you look up "lame" in the dictionary, it's eye opening. It means, "pathetically lacking in force and effectiveness." Think about that. If your advertising looks the same, and it's lame, then it's lacking force and effectiveness. If your marketing is lacking force and effectiveness, then it can't possibly deliver the kind of benefit or performance that you're looking for. It's basically impotent; it's a frustrating waste of time and money. If you've ever wondered why your advertising isn't pulling, this maybe a big part of it. It's also the reason you're constantly searching for new and different marketing gimmicks. Deep down you know that your marketing needs to be unique and different in order to help you stand out and attract customers. You just don't know how to do it. And we suspect you've also discovered that neither do any of the so-called advertising and marketing companies out there. They have no freakin' clue either. It's a classic case of the blind leading the blind, often ending with the "creative" people coming to you and asking, "What do you want to run this month?" Pathetic!

Imagine how cool it would be to have a constant stream of traffic-pulling ideas so that this cycle was broken once and for all. It's one of the ways we help our members make their lives more ESP—Enjoyable, Simple & Prosperous. We remove this burden of choice and deliver Snatcher-proof, creative promotions on a silver platter every single month, giving them freedom and confidence to live life and run their business on their own terms.

So now you know Same Is Lame, and that it is a complete waste of time, energy and cash to market and advertise the same way as every other dealer. That begs the question...how do you break the mold? How do you break away and look and sound completely different, be something totally unique?

In order to begin this process, you must answer two questions that are on the minds of all your prospects, whether they are intenders or non-intenders. And by the way, the great news here is that most dealerships are not addressing these questions in their marketing (or whatsoever), so when you enter the conversation and answer these questions, you can stand out and attract customers.

THE FIRST QUESTION
YOU MUST ANSWER

Would you say you provide pretty good customer service? Obviously, everybody SAYS they have good customer service. Wouldn't you agree?

Just about everyone says they sell quality vehicles at low prices too, right?

And there are plenty of dealerships that have been around for a long time, aren't there? So, without mentioning any of those things, can you tell us:

Why should a customer choose you over all other dealerships in your town?

It's almost an impossible question to answer for most dealerships. Usually dealers want to race to say, "Well, we've got a great selection. We've got excellent service. We have a wonderful location. We've been in business 75 years. We've got the lowest prices." The problem is that ALL dealers say that stuff. Have you ever seen a dealership offer poor selection, bad service, awful location and high prices? The reality is most customers don't care when you talk about that in your advertising. They EXPECT good service. They EXPECT quality vehicles. They EXPECT a good selection. Then they're let down when their expectations aren't met.

Now, simply, everyone is interested in price to some degree, and if given no other option or if all the options look the same, people will choose the cheaper option. If all things are equal then people will default to price as the primary differentiator. Dealers do a pretty pathetic job of differentiating one dealership from another, and the manufacturers add to the problem, because they want all dealerships to look the same. Think about advertising co-op or the building allowances they give you. What's it all designed to do? It's designed to homogenize—to cause you to look like every other dealership of the same make and for you to promote the big brand, not yourself. Are you starting to see the subtle clues of the Profit Snatchers' sinister plot? But don't worry. We won't let the chilly hand of the Snatchers choke out your unique spark of life.

Culturally, the car business has failed to differentiate itself dealership by dealership, so there remains no reason to choose one over the other, except price. So then, price becomes the chief motivator, the chief driving force, the only reason to choose. Plus, quite frankly, people are generally ignorant about most industries and product categories, and if they aren't ignorant, they are not confident about what they do know, so they default to the easiest and most natural reason to choose and compare...price.

This homogenization is currently going on with the move to online as well. You're seeing that dealerships, if they look the same in physical locations, then they look the same on the Internet as well, especially on sites where all you see is pictures of vehicles. Frankly, the vehicles are commodities and they are all the same. One Chevy Impala looks like another Chevy Impala except for a coat of paint, for the most part. The only things customers have to choose, at that point are features and price. Reality is, these people may think they're looking for the lowest price, but all the studies prove that price is always fifth or lower on the list of reasons why people choose to buy one product or service over another.

We also know that it is possible to differentiate yourself and cause people to choose you for reasons other than price (such as solutions, expertise, notoriety, special offers, security, celebrity and trust) and end up making a higher profit on every transaction. That's right, you will end up with more customers and a much higher profit than if you follow the traditional Same Is Lame automotive marketing model. Using Gravitational Marketing strategies, our members regularly sell more vehicles at higher gross profits and make more net profit in their stores month after month.

You know what is really interesting? Many dealers are lured into the low-price trap because they are following the herd. They are restricting themselves to selling only to the in-market buyers because they don't know how to attract anyone else.

The price-based, profit-slashing marketing they run further compounds the problem because the non-intenders aren't motivated by it and it only attracts the in-market, price conscious customer. It's a vicious self-perpetuating cycle.

Deep down, you know you haven't given prospects any good reason to choose you over any other dealer. You try, but the things you say fall on deaf ears because they have been said so many times and by now prospects are masters at filtering them, ignoring them, and in general, find them untrustworthy and irrelevant.

People usually don't believe claims about service, quality, or other generic items until after they've made a decision to buy from you and have personally experienced your dealership. Many people expect these things already from you and every other vendor they do business with and are viciously disappointed when they don't receive good customer service, guaranteed satisfaction, friendly, knowledgeable staff, a fair price, a great experience and a quality product. When they don't receive these things they feel betrayed and take it to management or worse, the Internet, to complain. If they assume these things are a given and only evaluate them after the transaction, do you think they will be motivated by advertising messages about them upfront? And when they are presented in the Same Is Lame style, you have about a snowball's chance in hell of motivating a virgin prospect.

Every day we help arm dealers to fight against the Snatchers. We give them the tools and weapons to protect themselves, their business, their profit and their lifestyle. When dealers like you use our methods, you experience firsthand that people will buy if you just give them a real, meaningful reason to choose you other than price. When you give people good reasons to choose you other than price and those reason are relevant, meaningful, emotional and helpful, sales increase, profits increase, and prices increase, too. Prices don't always have to go down. And what's crazy, and counterintuitive, is that CSI also goes up. Customers are more satisfied, because they have chosen you based on what they believe to be a more important reason. Because you've shown them you can deliver significant value. They've chosen to go with you for more important reasons other than price. Price is really only a last resort, best used when there's nothing else to choose from. When people don't know how to compare the options, they generally choose based on price.

We're sure you know the old saying that, "You get what you pay for," and people believe it to be true. So when they're paying less, they also feel like they are getting less. Sooner or later, the car dealership business is going to have to confront this and deal with this homogenization and Same Is Lame issue or be overtaken by a larger, less cost-heavy, but less valuable, middle man.

Of course, it's easier to just ignore that. And if you do, the Profit Snatchers will have their clawed fingers deep in your pockets once again.

THE RULE OF THIRDS

When you break free from price-based comparisons and you decide to differentiate with substance, you have a chance of becoming somebody's first choice. It's an opportunity you should take seriously because if you embrace this concept of becoming somebody's first choice, you will cause a flood of buyers to come forward and choose you. You'll have more buyers than you know what to do with, because you're finally giving people a reason that says, "My dealership is a better choice than all the other dealerships!"

To be someone's first choice, you have to follow what we call the "Rule Of Thirds." The function of the rule is to polarize people and create a group of raving fans. In order to accomplish this you will have to be off-putting to some people. Let's call it a third of the people, roughly, and about a third of the people will generally be indifferent about what you do. But that final third will be ecstatic about what you do. They'll be drawn to you. They'll love you. It's Gravitational Marketing at work. Buyers will be pulled toward you as if by a natural force. They will be attracted to your message and drawn to you for your uniqueness.

There's a perfect example of this principle in action in North Carolina. One of our oldest members runs an independent dealership there, and has received national recognition for being such an unusual personality. He occasionally receives emails from people in his market telling him they'd never buy a car from him. But he thanks them for their honesty and feedback, and keeps on going. And it works for him. He just emailed the group announcing that last month was the best month in his history, up 33% from last year, which was also a record. He sells more cars every month at his used car dealership than most new car stores sell in their best month. And he often turns those "Negative Nellies" into happy buyers.

Most dealerships are trying to be all things to all people, catering to everyone, so you know what that makes them? That makes them everybody's fourth or fifth choice. They don't really mean much to anyone because their message doesn't resonate. It doesn't polarize. It doesn't turn anyone off and it doesn't turn anyone on, so nobody pays attention.

You can't succeed in business or life that way, so you have to be willing to abandon part of the people, to be off-putting to a third. We've very successfully used this strategy for ourselves and many other business owners and dealers over the years. We know there are people reading this right now who have closed the book, moved on with their life and said, "This is not for me. These guys are not for me." Maybe it was the cover, maybe our writing style, our frankness, our position or our ideas. Whatever it was, they just didn't like us and that's okay. It happens every day for us and we intentionally do and say things and act ways that cause people to turn the other way and run for the hills. Far enough away to be safe from us crazy guys with the non-traditional ideas about making big profit in the car business. If we're not a fit for you, you're not a fit for us and it's best that we probably don't do any business together. That's how we look at it and that's how you have to look at it if you want to naturally attract a load of customers and escape the Snatchers' grip.

CHAPTER 8:

CREATING ACTION—NOW

H ere's a bit of harsh reality: none of this matters one bit unless people actually peel their butts off their couches and come to the dealership to BUY A CAR. There's too much confusion these days about name recognition, brand awareness, top of mind, search position, reviews, frequency, etc. It's ALL important, but the only thing that counts is when someone shows up. Agreed?

So, we've answered the first question, "Why should somebody choose you?" and now let's move on to answering the second question, which speaks directly to this critical element:

"Why should somebody choose you right now?"

This is a very important follow-up to the first question. First of all, "Why should they choose you?" and second of all, "Why should they choose you right now?" See, you need to sell cars now (and later), not just later.

THE "SOMETHING FOR NOTHING" ASPIRATION

Have you ever stood back in a casino and looked out over the sea of blue hair at the slot machines, wondering what these people are chasing after? Why do they stay up all night, bleary-eyed, just plunking quarters mindlessly into the machine, pulling the handle and losing cash when they have no extra cash to spare?

Or have you ever been in the high-rollers room to witness wealthy men and women separate themselves from tens or hundreds of thousands of dollars in under five minutes?

What drives this craziness?

There's a secret psychological trigger that affects almost everybody: people have what we call a "something for nothing" aspiration. That is, most people are programmed to desperately want to get something for nothing. This is why in 2010 alone Americans spent $49 billion playing the lottery and Vegas made $10 billion dollars in profit. Horse racing, sports betting, game shows, real estate investing, buy-one-get-one-free sales, extreme couponing and Obamacare. These are just a few additional examples of the aspiration at work. When you think about it like that you realize how far reaching and powerful this trigger really is.

It affects us all to some degree. No one is immune to it. Smart people, dumb people, tall people, short people...rich, poor, good credit, bad credit. It gets us all.

What we're about to reveal to you is extremely sensitive, and can be used for good or for evil. Our preference, of course, is that you use it only for good. In fact, if you're a shady dealer who rips people off and steals their money and sells garbage cars, well, maybe you oughta' just take a hike and skip the rest of this book all together.

So, now that it's just us well-intentioned folks, let's continue.

It is possible, even advisable, to leverage the "Something For Nothing" aspiration in your effort to attract customers and cause people to choose you right now. There's nothing dirty about it. It's the driving force behind all sales. But it's important that you understand the science behind it so you can maximize the effects of the application.

What it boils down to is this: all special offers tickle customers' greed glands. If you want to capitalize on the "Something For Nothing" psychological trigger, you need to properly make special offers. We'll show you how.

There's an excellent example of this at work recently in the car business...just look at "Cash For Clunkers." When people were given the opportunity to trade in their worthless junker for $4,500, they sprang into action. In total, 690,000 cars were sold under the program. How many of these people do you think were in the market before "Cash For Clunkers?"

In fact, the vast majority of those cars were sold to people who weren't in the market before the promotion. They were accelerated into the market, converted from non-intender to buyer, driven by their "Something For Nothing" aspiration.

The promotion had nothing to do with the in-market shoppers because it didn't talk about price or vehicles or features. Even though it had nothing to do with price or vehicles, the market went from selling a few cars to selling a whole bunch of cars in the short period that "Cash For Clunkers" was active, so where did all these buyers come from?

They were motivated into the market, not by price or vehicle selection, but by something else entirely. They were motivated by a special offer that had the power to solve a problem.

Specifically there were three big elements to the "Cash For Clunkers" offer that made it so effective. These elements caused the market to react rapidly and dramatically.

If you want the market to react rapidly to the offers you make, you'll want to be sure to include these same three elements.

This may be the biggest tactical take-away from this entire book.

THE TRIFECTA OF DRAMATIC, RAPID RESPONSE

Here's the formula:

Scarcity + Urgency + Believability =
Dramatic, Rapid Response

Scarcity is when there's a limit to the number of people who can take advantage of the offer you're making.

Urgency is when there is a limited amount of time to take advantage of the offer.

Believability is when the customer believes it's true. Important to note, just because it is true doesn't mean they'll believe it. There's a huge difference between believability and truth. They work best when combined, but don't confuse them and try to substitute one for the other. Your offers should be true and believable.

So why does this work?

Experience shows that when you create a deadline (urgency), when you give people a time frame in which they have to respond, response dramatically increases!

Most car dealers don't understand this fact and miss putting deadlines and reasons to act now into their marketing. People are terrified of missing the opportunity. Fear of loss is always a stronger motivator than the potential for gain.

"Cash For Clunkers" had urgency because there was an end date.

Same concept is at work with scarcity. People are worried you'll run out before they get there, so they rush to get their fair share.

"Cash For Clunkers" had scarcity because there were limited funds.

But it's all worthless without believability. "Cash For Clunkers" had believability because it was backed by the federal government. However, there's a much easier way to create believability, a way you can control: presenting a reason why.

Simply put, a reason why is exactly what it sounds like. It's a reason why you're making an offer. The vast majority of all offers made in retail advertising miss this completely. Customers are inclined to believe, despite their "Something For Nothing" aspiration, that most advertising is false advertising. Special offers are generally suspect because they exist in a vacuum. For instance, "50% Off! Because..." There's no reason, so people are skeptical. Especially when the offer is coming from a car dealer.

There's a tremendous opportunity for car dealers to forget about nonsense offers that have no basis in reality, and start finding real reasons to make real special offers. A truthful and believable offer with a truthful and believable reason why is one of the most powerful marketing elements in existence.

If customers don't believe your offer, they're unlikely to peel themselves away from the boob tube. Lotteries and casinos need occasional (regular) winners. Network marketing needs success stories. Special offers from car dealers need a truthful and believable reason why. It is what it is.

In the car business there is a proliferation of advertisers who know enough about marketing to realize they need to create a sales promotion just like many retail outlets do, and they give that sales promotion a name, like

"March Madness" or "Monster Sale" that ties into something generic. Maybe the promotion even has some kind of urgency to it, like "This Week Only!" but again, it has no believability. It's so cliché. Overdone. The promotion is so incredibly transparent that it embodies SAME IS LAME! It's irrelevant. You may already be aware of the increase in traffic that can come from using these tricks of scarcity, urgency and believability, but unless you've dived in completely and created some real believability in your marketing, you haven't experienced the power of it.

"Cash For Clunkers" had such powerful believability because the government basically endorsed it.

"Cash For Clunkers" wasn't just some car-dealer hype or gimmick. It was a real deal that was going on. Now, what we've discovered is that you can make a "Cash For Clunkers"-like phenomenon occur every single month by making real offers and expressing the reason for the offer. Imagine yourself standing in your showroom with people lining up, people who woke up in the morning with absolutely no intention of buying a car that day, and now these people are there asking for your help. They're lining up and seeking a solution only you can provide and they're not sensitive to price. You'll sell more cars than you'd ever imagined you could, and soon realize an average gross profit that is higher than it's ever been. This is not a fantasy. This is a constant reality every single day for our clients.

If you decide to do this on your own, you have to get creative and come up with new ways to explain WHY you're having a sale or making a special offer and you have to do it every single month in a fresh, fun and relevant way. For instance, if you're offering to pay more than a trade is worth (like the "Cash For Clunkers" offer) you must explain why you would do such a thing. Is it because there aren't enough used cars to go around or because used car prices are rising at the auction? If you're going to cut the price on a specific vehicle, why? Is it because you received more than you ordered? Or is there a space constraint?

Given a reasonable explanation why you would offer "something for nothing" most people would be more than happy to rush to receive your offer.

Of course the Profit Snatchers don't want you to know this little secret and they surely don't want you to be armed with the tools to accomplish such a mission. They want you to be defenseless, on your back, revealing your soft underbelly with low price as your only cover. This way you're an easy kill later when they want your territory, feel you're no longer an asset or are done with dealers all together.

CHAPTER 9:

QUIT THE CAR BUSINESS

By now you're beginning to realize the true power of the method we're describing and starting to understand what makes it tick. But let's pause.

We often ask dealers if they are open-minded and willing to try things they haven't done before. We ask them to take a chance and be open to something new, and frequently they say yes, but sometimes, we find that they aren't really open to change. They are just saying they are. They're fooling themselves.

The solutions we are about to show you are for dealers who are willing to try something new, to truly get out of their own way and do something that can make an enormous impact. The results, for many of our members, are increases that are staggering and life-transforming.

Upon joining our community, one import dealer from Missouri told us he couldn't afford to vacation with his family, and less than a year later, while attending one of our quarterly meetings in Orlando, he told us, "After this meeting, I'm going to be spending a week with my family here in Orlando. My dealership is running smoothly and I have no worries about that, and I have made more money than I have in the past several years in just this short amount of time I've been with you. At one point I didn't think I'd ever take a vacation again." That's a powerful transformation and something that we're very proud of, because that is why we do what we do. That same man has gone on now to take four months off from the dealership (while it went on to have the best four months in its history) to help rebuild schools, houses and churches in towns devastated by tornadoes. That's one very brief story from our stack of hundreds. We share it with you to get your attention. You can't afford not to take this very seriously.

THE THIRD BIG PROBLEM

Let's examine the third—and final—big reason traffic and sales are depressed, and let's solve it. This third big problem is commoditization.

What is commoditization? It's the act in which your business, your dealership, your life blood becomes attacked and assimilated by the Snatchers as they turn you from something special into a generic, unoriginal and boring commodity. A commodity is exactly what the Snatchers want you to be. Just take a look. The definition of commoditization is "the dilution of a market sector's internal differentiation and competitive nuances in favor of a mass market, where price alone determines consumer behavior." Or, if you prefer an alternate definition, "a good or service whose wide availability typically leads to smaller profit margins and diminishes the importance of factors (like brand, services, solutions, expertise and relationship) other than price."

How about that? That's exactly what we are examining here. What's the push from the manufacturers and some other industry insiders, which we won't mention by name here? Diluting the sector's internal differentiation. And in this case, it's not the differentiation of the vehicles themselves, it's the differentiation of the dealerships themselves. Of course, cars are commodities. They already have very little differentiation other than price, except for the fringe vehicles. But the big sellers are all trying to round the cars off to be conservative and be a fit for most people.

The Profit Snatchers want to round you all off, too. The manufacturers want all the dealerships to look the same. If they have their druthers, a customer's experience buying a car from one XYZ franchise dealership would be no different than when buying a car at another XYZ franchise dealership across town. We don't blame the manufacturers for wanting this. But is it in YOUR best interest?

We're not going to tell you that the manufacturers want you to fail, but there are some big questions that have to be answered here about the true motivation. Have you ever felt pressure, from internal or external forces, to lose your internal differentiation? Have you ever noticed the undercurrent in the industry toward a state where price alone determines consumer behavior? Absolutely! It's going on right now. This move and definition of commoditization and the realization of it in the car business is scary, isn't it?

It's terrifying, frankly, and a huge problem. But fortunately for you, this is a problem that you can overcome yourself. It's not outside the capability of you or any other dealership. You don't have to be a genius. The solution has already been invented. And, even though your situation and dealership is unique, the path has been blazed for you. All you have to do is follow in the footsteps of other people who've done it before you, and by the way, here's the first key.

STOP SELLING CARS, START SELLING SOLUTIONS

Take a moment and let that sink in.

Stop selling cars and start selling solutions. Solutions are what people seek every day. Our lives are hectic. We have no time. We are stressed. We are frustrated. We've got problems. Can you identify with all of that?

What people are looking for are solutions to those problems, to those stresses and frustrations, to the things that are wasting their time. They're looking for a solution to make them feel better, to make their pain go away, and sometimes a purchase of something that they're emotionally tied to, something that they see as a representation of themselves, does a lot toward solving a problem or making a desire come true. When you start selling that, when your marketing is about that, not prices and vehicles, you then can tap that 98 percent and start talking to them, which drives a ton more traffic!

This is the whole key. The key to selling a lot more cars and getting you a lot more profit and making your customers a lot happier and more willing to refer and come back for service. This is what Gravitational Marketing is about: showing you how to stand out and sell more without spending more and driving buyers, who come back for service and refer repeatedly.

We aren't going to say that price isn't important to customers because clearly it is. We've all felt that there is price sensitivity, these days perhaps even more than in normal times, but we would suggest that low price is far less valuable than solutions. When you think about it, there is a lot of talk about value and most people assume that means lowering prices. The interesting thing about value is that value is as valuable as it is; this means the less valuable something is, the lower the price is and the more valuable it is, the higher the price is. Solutions rank much higher in people's minds in value than price alone does. ANYBODY can sell something for the lowest price. No skill required. It's not so common to find someone who really cares, who will really help and who really adds value. More on this soon.

Customers only turn to price when there are no other factors to consider and when there's really nothing else to choose by. So if someone can solve your problem or some product or service can solve your problem, that has much greater value and you're willing to pay more.

Now you can radically change the type of customer and the type of process by which you sell cars and the process by which you attract customers, by increasing your value proposition, by focusing on being a solutions provider.

Before we move on any further, we ask you to suspend your disbelief, to put aside your fear of the unknown, your fear of trying new things and ask you to step outside your comfort zone. Be open to something completely different that may seem a little radical, and something that could very well change the course of your business for the better. This, in turn, could change the course of your life for the better, by making you more profit and giving your customers more of what they want, making them happier, and by allowing you to have more time to spend with your friends and family doing the things that you love to do, adding more ESP to your life. If you're open to that, then you are ready to grasp the solutions we're presenting in this book, and ready to receive the answers to the questions you have about creating more traffic and more sales.

PRODUCT PUSHER VS. TRUSTED ADVISOR

You may be asking yourself, "Guys, how do I actually apply this? How do I take these foundations, these ideas, these principles, and actually use them in my business to make a difference?"

First of all, a very practical solution is to become a trusted advisor, instead of simply being a product-pusher. When you place your ads with prices and payments, when you upload your cars to inventory listing sites, you're a product-pusher. The Sears ad with the washer and dryer is product-pushing. We are encouraging you to provide solutions, help and advice, instead of simply being a product-pusher who's just worried about merchandising the next vehicle and thinking about what price to put on the windshield or the web site.

It's rare to find a trusted advisor who is willing to solve your problems. People gladly pay top dollar to trusted advisors, but they haggle over nickels with merchants.

Being a trusted advisor means being there for your customers, whether they are ready to buy or not. Be there with answers, solutions and help. One of the ways you can do that, a very practical way, is to create helpful information that addresses fears, concerns, and problems that people have when buying a car. We've written many special reports and books with our clients and we're constantly pushing our clients and anyone we meet in the auto business to take the step to become an author.

You're probably already aware of the fact that in American society people who write books, authors, command a level of credibility above and beyond most ordinary people. Just watch any daytime talk show or evening news program. Who do they have on as guests? Experts and authors. People who have books. And it doesn't have to take a lifetime to put a book together. This is advice you can implement immediately. Hire an interviewer to ask you questions that would be helpful to customers. Record the interview, then have it transcribed. Send the transcription to an editor who will turn it into prose. Hire a graphic designer to design a book cover and page layout. There are even companies out there who provide a turnkey service, like www.48hrbooks.com or www.advantagefamily.com that will do it all for you. You can sell your book on www.amazon.com or host a big book signing event at the dealership. Offer an autographed copy to everyone who takes a test drive. Do you see where this is going? You're no longer a car dealer, you're an expert! Big difference.

We give our members multiple ways to become instant authors, experts, thought-leaders and celebrities. We show them simple and immediate methods of leveraging information, technology and the written word to differentiate themselves and stand out. With our systems and strategies anyone can harness the persuasive power of experts and authors even if they've never written a single word or done anything like it before.

It is entirely possible to transcend the typical car dealer and the Same Is Lame mentality. When you think about it, there really is so much emphasis on the Internet these days in selling cars that most people are treating it just like most other advertising. Dealers are throwing up a bunch of vehicles with prices and gimmicky sales. In contrast, our members use a web site that we create for them that doesn't even feature vehicles.

Many of our members use the Internet to position themselves as experts, as trusted advisors who deliver value to the market, to their customer base and to the community at large. Online you can offer special reports for download or create a video blog that people can watch regularly for education and entertainment. This information will set you apart in your market as a trusted advisor rather than a tin pusher.

Many of the videos that our dealers put out there have nothing really to do with the car business. These videos center around the dealers themselves—they're personal.

They tap into the emotions of the customers, focusing on their personal lives, their philosophical beliefs, etc. When you share yourself with people, you forge connections and when that connection happens, you start creating customers for life.

Then you sell more cars. You make more money because people buy from people they know, like and trust. They're going to buy from a friend in the car business before they buy from someone they don't know in the car business. So start positioning yourself as their friend in the car business.

When you do that on a mass scale, you get mass sales. For example, a number of our members have found a tremendous benefit from being picked up in the local media and on occasion in the national media. We frequently create press releases for our members that they distribute to local media. Surprisingly, many times the local news wants to do a story on what the dealer is up to at their dealership and in their community. Some of our clients have made it on national cable news, Fox News and Fox Business, as expert contributors.

Don't think that just because you're in the car business you're limited to being a car dealer. Better to be an expert who also runs a car dealership than a merchant who runs a car dealership.

SWITCH FROM ADVERTISING TO CONTENT

Do you remember the principle of SAME IS LAME? Let's apply it to your advertising. It's one of the simplest and most immediate things you can do—make your marketing look like something other than all the other car ads, make your dealership stand out as special and unique.

Let's discuss our style of advertising, for example. Our ads don't necessarily look or sound like other car ads. Ironically, most of the ads we create don't even show cars or prices. Our ads are striking and look important! They're not retail looking, washer and dryer style ads. It is important to note that our approach is what we call "media-agnostic," meaning we're not more fond of or more favorable toward one media than any other. We use the most practical and efficient media at your disposal, at our disposal, for any member at any given time. It's really something that's very specific to the media available to you, the market opportunities, choices, constraints and scenarios, so it's a custom approach in terms of the type of media, but not in terms of the way to craft the message itself.

Consider this: people read the paper for the stories, not the ads. People watch TV to be entertained, not to be sold. People search the Internet for information, not for pop-ups. People read their email to communicate, not to look at spam. People listen to the radio for music or talk, not to hear ads.

When we emphasize making your marketing look or sound like something other than car ads, it's also helpful to make your advertising look like something other than advertising, period. In print, use advertorials (ads that look like articles). Online, use information. On the radio, sound like a personality. Why? Because the 98 percent who aren't shopping will never pay attention to a car ad. When they see an ad that has cars, prices and payments, they get all they need in a nanosecond. They can skip that. But if your ads look like content, people will give them a chance. If your case is well presented, they'll consume the whole message. If your advertisements address the solutions, the problems, the fears, concerns, hopes, dreams and desires that the customers have that are unrelated to the car business but then loop back into the car business, you have a fighting chance of bringing them into your dealership.

You're going to be flat-out amazed when you find out how much additional traffic and sales can be produced by running advertising that looks completely different than all the other car ads...ads that stand out and address solutions. It's dramatic.

CHAPTER 10:

THE BATTLE BEGINS

By now you're loaded for bear. The ideas, methods and strategies we've shared with you are so powerful and potent, perhaps beyond comprehension.

We want to advise you: do not try any of these strategies unless you are committed to the results that can be generated when you do something like this. This stuff works. But it's a double-edged sword. You need to be prepared to handle the traffic and be committed to providing value, not just selling the lowest price. It's harder work, but it's more fun and more rewarding. Preparation is the key.

It's best to be guided by someone who understands how to use these principles and by someone who has used them effectively in the past. Get connected with a group of like-minded dealers who will share ideas and compare notes. You'll learn and grow faster when you learn and grow with others.

Finally, don't use these strategies until you're ready to have a business and life that are Enjoyable, Simple & Prosperous...ready to have a crowd of people who believe in you and view you as a trusted advisor, as an expert in the community and as a leader in the community. Be ready to make more profit in 12 months than you've made in the last 12 years.

Think of how relieved you'll feel and how happy you'll be when you've made some simple, turnkey changes and you realize that you are known and respected in your marketplace, more people know you than ever before and people are paying attention. You'll have more money coming in the doors than ever before, but most importantly, you're actually spending time with your family and enjoying life. You're understanding and appreciating the essence of life and realizing that every moment we have is precious and important and perfect. When you experience what it's like to watch each moment go by and not have stress, to be comfortable, that's probably the biggest payoff there is.

That is the biggest benefit people realize between six months to a year after doing this. They come back and say, "Guys, we sold cars. We made money. Everything's been fantastic. However, the really big thing is I enjoyed myself and enjoyed life; I had fun in the process. I've made money before and never realized that I could have fun doing it and enjoy life." In fact, those were words used by one of our longest-term members, an independent dealer from Kentucky.

As you consider the benefits of this approach, of using creative that transcends typical retail car advertising, that makes you stand out and sell more without spending more, that sets you apart and makes you a trusted advisor in your community, then you might like to think about how this could impact the way people in your community look at you. Think about the way your employees will look at you, the way your family will view you, and about the way your life might change for the better when you become seen as somebody who sets a standard for an entire industry and for a community, rather than just being a car dealer.

You can't change the stereotype that's been set for dealers over years of negativity, but you can change yourself and the way your community perceives you—not as an industry but as an individual.

Imagine being immune to the Profit Snatchers. Ahhh...relief. Their slimy tentacles just can't get a grip on dealers who embrace these ideals, who use these methods. It's doubtful that we can banish the Profit Snatchers from the industry completely. They'll always be there, hovering over dealers, siphoning profit, opportunity and independence from the weak-willed, uninformed and those who fail to seek a better solution.

But now you're armed, you're informed and you've demonstrated your willingness to seek out real solutions. You no longer have to sell on price alone. You no longer have to sacrifice profit. You no longer have to hide in the shadow of a negative reputation. You no longer have to be ashamed. You no longer have to be a victim. In us, you have found the solution. Now the battle begins. HOOYA! Let's mount up, soldiers, and go to war.

There's no limit to what the Profit Snatchers can do. They could destroy the Earth. If anything should happen to us you must go to Gort, you must say these words, "Klaatu, barada nikto." Please repeat that.

AFTERWORD:
HOW TO BECOME R.I.C.H.

This is strong stuff, which is all accomplished through the RICH acronym. Some people think Rich Dealers is all about making more money, but in fact, that's only part of the equation. RICH is an acronym that stands for "a Respected, Influential, Contributor, who Helps People and Has Fun." A Rich Dealer is a dealer who's respected in their local community as a thought leader, as someone who makes an impact and a difference. A Rich Dealer is someone who's influential in his or her area and causes changes, and who has power and is a contributor. A dealer who gives back to the community, to the people around him and the world in general, leaving more than he or she takes, and finally, has fun doing this because if it's not fun, frankly, it's probably not worth doing.

Has it ever occurred to you that by making a few simple changes in your marketing, as we've just described, you could become a market leader who stands head and shoulders above the rest and is an example for others to follow?

Really there is a very formulaic approach to these lofty ideals, a step-by-step blueprint to the whole thing that you should know about. It's beyond the scope of this book to cover in detail. It's a rabbit hole that goes deeper than most could ever imagine. We can take you there, if you'd like.

Here's what other dealers have realized about us. We're two young, aggressive guys. We have been doing this for over a decade, though, and have netted a significant amount of experience. But most important, we're magnets. Magnets of information, of wisdom, of input, of other people's experience, of success and of money. We spend more than a hundred thousand dollars every year on our own personal education. We're connected with some of the top minds in Internet marketing and direct marketing. We network with business-owners and entrepreneurs all over the world who are running hugely successful businesses, not just in the car business. We purposely look outside the car business to work with entrepreneurs to learn their businesses, which we bring back into our business, because most ideas in the car business are just rehashed rip-offs of old ideas, the same old nonsense getting regurgitated over and over again.

Organizations recognize us as being different. We've been asked to speak on Internet marketing and leveraging social media in Dubai, London and Paris. Dozens of magazines and newspapers have published our marketing concepts because people realize that our ideas are innovative and challenging. Our methods are unique to most business niches, because again, the typical ideas are all boring and unoriginal. We bring fresh eyes, fresh ears and fresh perspective on things because of the volume of information we consume and because of our connections.

Bottom line, we've got a formula for doing all this, and we can do it for you and make it fast and simple. Or you can do it yourself using the methods we've laid out in this book.

WHAT'S NEXT?

If you feel like you're the kind of person who would benefit from being connected with us and with other like-minded dealers, this is the time to get involved and this is the group to get involved with.

Our members are seekers, winners. Our group is immune to the Profit Snatchers. We are the men who can help you, and you will love us for it. That sounds a little strange, but it happens for our members all the time.

We understand how you feel, perhaps a little overwhelmed. Many of the dealers who we've talked to have felt this way. They found that once they started down this path, the car business became fun again. They start by dipping their toes in the water, utilizing our creative ideas and running our campaigns, and thinking about providing solutions and becoming an expert. After they implement these ideas they see a substantial and immediate increase in leads, opportunities, traffic, sales and profit. But it doesn't stop there.

As our members go deeper and further implement our ideas and strategies, they come back and tell us, "You know what? The car business is fun again. You've re-energized me. I've found that spark again. I enjoy going to work every day now, and it's all thanks to you guys and the connection with this group. Thank you." That's an actual message sent to us by one of our members, and we receive messages just like this nearly every week. This is what makes us come to work every day. This is the kind of community we set out to create; we've succeeded.

This isn't just about selling stuff to car dealers and making money because of it. That's not what we are about. We believe there are too many moochers in this business...people and companies who add little to no value to dealers, but exist only for their own profit.

We're here to make an impact. Don't get us wrong, we want to make money, too. We are businessmen and entrepreneurs and, as such, we like to make money. Money is a way to keep score, a way to help others and a way to measure our success. But what we're really about is making an impact and that's what our company does. It makes an impact on dealers, dealers' families, people who work at dealerships, the customers of the dealerships and ultimately, it makes an impact on the communities in which our members live.

Car dealerships are among the largest local businesses in most communities and as such, dealers have the ability to make a big impact on their community. Many of our members turn out to be major contributors in their towns once they finally get their business operating at a consistently profitable level. When we help you succeed, your success makes the lives of so many people better, and that's precisely what we are all about.

Ninety days from now, when you're effortlessly selling more cars, seeing more traffic, seeing your gross profit increase, having more fun in the car business, going home earlier, experiencing less stress and spending more time with your family—and not just spending time with your family, but being present with your family, really being there with them instead of being somewhere else in your mind, being there in mind, body and spirit—at that moment, you're going to look back to this day and remember reading this and say to yourself, "I'm glad I stuck it through, and I'm glad I made the decision I did." This is a transformational moment.

The next step is to talk to a Rich Dealers Advisor. These are people who have been trained personally by us. They're experts at implementing these principles at stores like yours. If you've already been speaking to a Rich Dealers advisor, get back in touch with them now.

Your Rich Dealers Advisor can answer all your questions and help you more fully understand the process and the program. They can introduce you to other dealers who have successfully made this transition and help you make a rapid and smooth transition yourself.

We do only work with one dealer in a market area, so if your market is unavailable, please accept our apologies. But we do strongly encourage you to implement the ideas and methods we've shared in this book. You'll be glad you did.

In closing, thank you. Thank you for your time and your attention, which is valuable and precious. Our goal was to provide usable, practical and realistic advice that you can use and profit from. Hopefully we have accomplished our mission.

—Jimmy Vee & Travis Miller

Learn more or contact us at:

www.RichDealers.com

407-275-8667

CPSIA information can be obtained at www.ICGtesting.com
Printed in the USA
LVOW10*1139101014

408147LV00004B/7/P